J B Wade
DiPrimio, Pete
Dwyane Wade

$18.50
ocn706025186
04/24/2012

A Robbie Reader

# DWYANE WADE

Pete DiPrimio

MIAMI

3

**Mitchell Lane**
PUBLISHERS

P.O. Box 196
Hockessin, Delaware 19707
Visit us on the web: www.mitchelllane.com
Comments? email us: mitchelllane@mitchelllane.com

### Mitchell Lane
PUBLISHERS

Printing    1      2      3      4      5      6      7      8      9

## A Robbie Reader Biography

| | | |
|---|---|---|
| Abigail Breslin | Dr. Seuss | Mia Hamm |
| Adrian Peterson | Dwayne "The Rock" Johnson | Miley Cyrus |
| Albert Einstein | **Dwyane Wade** | Miranda Cosgrove |
| Albert Pujols | Dylan & Cole Sprouse | Philo Farnsworth |
| Alex Rodriguez | Eli Manning | Raven-Symoné |
| Aly and AJ | Emily Osment | Roy Halladay |
| AnnaSophia Robb | Emma Watson | Selena Gomez |
| Amanda Bynes | Hilary Duff | Shaquille O'Neal |
| Ashley Tisdale | Jaden Smith | Story of Harley-Davidson |
| Brenda Song | Jamie Lynn Spears | Sue Bird |
| Brittany Murphy | Jennette McCurdy | Syd Hoff |
| Charles Schulz | Jesse McCartney | Taylor Lautner |
| Chris Johnson | Jimmie Johnson | Tiki Barber |
| Cliff Lee | Johnny Gruelle | Tim Lincecum |
| Dakota Fanning | Jonas Brothers | Tom Brady |
| Dale Earnhardt Jr. | Jordin Sparks | Tony Hawk |
| David Archuleta | Justin Beiber | Troy Polamalu |
| Demi Lovato | Keke Palmer | Victoria Justice |
| Donovan McNabb | Larry Fitzgerald | |
| Drake Bell & Josh Peck | LeBron James | |

**Library of Congress Cataloging-in-Publication Data**
DiPrimio, Pete.
  Dwyane Wade / by Pete DiPrimio.
    p. cm. — (A robbie reader)
  Includes bibliographical references and index.
  ISBN 978-1-61228-063-9 (library bound)
  1. Wade, Dwyane, 1982– – Juvenile literature. 2. Basketball players — United States — Biography — Juvenile literature. I. Title.
  GV884.W23D47 2011
  796.323092 — dc23
  [B]
                                                                                                2011016785

**eBook ISBN:** 9781612281742

**ABOUT THE AUTHOR:** Pete DiPrimio is a veteran sports columnist for the *Fort Wayne* [Indiana] *News-Sentinel* and a longtime freelance feature, fiction, and travel writer. He's also an adjunct lecturer for the National Sports Journalism Center at IUPU-Indianapolis. He is the author of three nonfiction books pertaining to Indiana University athletics, and of *Tom Brady, Eli Manning, Drew Brees, How'd They Do That in Ancient Rome?, The Sphinx, The Supreme Court,* and *We Visit Iran* for Mitchell Lane Publishers.

**PUBLISHER'S NOTE:** The following story has been thoroughly researched and to the best of our knowledge represents a true story. While every possible effort has been made to ensure accuracy, the publisher will not assume liability for damages caused by inaccuracies in the data, and makes no warranty on the accuracy of the information contained herein. This story has not been authorized or endorsed by Dwyane Wade.

# TABLE OF CONTENTS

Words in **bold** type can be found in the glossary.

Miami's Dwyane Wade (left) and Shaquille O'Neal celebrate after the team won the 2006 NBA championship. Shaq called Wade the "greatest in the universe." Others called him "a poor man's Michael Jordan."

# Better Than Jordan?

In the 2006 **NBA** finals, the Miami Heat was in big trouble against the Dallas Mavericks. Dallas won the first two games of the best-of-seven series. The Mavs needed just two more victories to win the **championship** (CHAM-pee-un-ship).

But Miami had Dwyane Wade, playing the best basketball of his career with what his college coach called "controlled rage." A week or so earlier he had led the Heat over the Detroit Pistons in the **conference** (KON-fruntz) finals. He overcame the flu and a stay in the hospital to score 14 points. That win was huge, because Detroit had knocked Miami out of the **playoffs** the year before.

But Dallas was a bigger, better team than Detroit. It beat Miami twice in Dallas. Then the series switched to Miami for three games. The Heat needed to win at least two games to have a chance.

Miami also had Shaquille O'Neal, one of the greatest centers in NBA history. He had won three NBA titles with the Los Angeles Lakers before he was traded to the Heat.

Still, this was Wade's team. He was the star and Shaq knew it. By the end of the series, so would Dallas.

The Mavs were leading Game 3 by 13 points with less than seven minutes to go. Then Wade took over. He scored 15 points in the fourth quarter, 12 of them in the last six minutes. He finished with 42 points, and the Heat won 98-96.

Now they had a chance.

Heat players were so confident in Wade that, as Miami backup center Alonzo Mourning said in his book **Resilience** (ree-ZIL-yuntz), they just waited for D-Wade to save them.

He did. He had 36 points in Game 4, and Miami won 98-74. The Heat won Game 5 in overtime, 101-100, with Wade scoring 43 points and making the two game-winning **free throws** with 1.1 seconds left.

The series went back to Dallas with Miami leading three games to two. The Mavs needed to win the final two games to win the series, but Wade never gave them a chance. He had 36 points in Game 6, and Miami won 95-92 for its first NBA title.

Wade **averaged** (AV-rijd) 39.2 points and 8.3 **rebounds** over the final four games. For the series it was 34.7 points and 7.8 rebounds. Some experts consider this the greatest performance ever in an NBA finals series— better than Michael Jordan, better than Shaq, better than anybody.

Wade was voted most valuable player (MVP) of the 2006 championship series

Dwyane had it tough growing up in Chicago. His sister Tragil (left) helped raise him. She also helped their mother, Jolinda (right), overcome a lot of problems. Jolinda is now very big in Dwyane's life.

# Early Years

Dwyane Tyrone Wade Jr. was born on January 17, 1982, on the South Side of Chicago. His parents, Dwyane Sr. and Jolinda, divorced soon after. Dwyane lived with his mother for a while, but their neighborhood was full of drugs and gangs. They often did not have enough to eat. Jolinda got into drugs and was rarely around. Dwyane's older sister, Tragil, stepped in to raise him. Things got so bad he moved across town with his father, a former U.S. Army sergeant, and stepmother, Bessie McDaniel. They soon moved to Robbins, Illinois.

Robbins is near Chicago, and Dwyane was a Chicago Bulls fan. He tried to play like his favorite player, superstar Michael Jordan.

Dwyane played for Harold L. Richards High School in Oak Lawn. He didn't play much at first, partly because his stepbrother, Demetris McDaniel, was the star.

Dwyane had a great junior season. Over the summer, he had grown four inches taller, and he'd worked hard on his skills. As a senior he led his team to a 24-5 record. He set a school record for points (676) and steals (106) in a season.

In his senior year, he really got noticed when he scored 48 and 42 points in a pair of December games. He also drew attention because of his character. The high school football coach told Marquette coach Tom Crean that, in 27 years, Dwyane was one of the three finest kids he'd ever seen at the school who didn't play for him.

Dwyane was eight years old when he went to live with his father, Dwyane Sr.

Dwyane had great **potential** (poh-TEN-shul), but his grades were not the greatest, and his college test score was one point too low to allow him to play college basketball. Only three colleges **recruited** (ree-KROO-ted) him: Marquette, Illinois State, and DePaul. For his first year, he would not be able to play. He would have to study hard and get good grades. If not, he would never be able to play college ball.

Crean and Marquette believed in Dwyane. Crean said he took what the football coach said to heart. He had gotten to know Dwyane as a person and was very impressed. He pushed Marquette officials to take a chance on him.

In the end, Crean's support made the difference. Dwyane signed with Marquette.

The Marquette Golden Eagle

People knew Dwyane was good coming into college, but they didn't know how good. He quickly showed them. In his first year at Marquette, he averaged 17.8 points, 6.6 rebounds, 3.4 assists, and 2.5 steals.

## CHAPTER THREE

# Instant Impact

Wade hit the books hard his first year at Marquette and became **eligible** (EL-ih-jih-bul) to play the next season. He made an instant impact. He led the Golden Eagles in scoring and Conference USA in **steals**. Marquette went 26-7, its best record since 1993–94.

He was even better the next year. He averaged 21.5 points per game, set a school single-season record with 710 points, and led the Golden Eagles to a 27-6 record and the Conference USA title. For the first time since 1977, Marquette would play in the **NCAA Tournament**'s (TUR-nuh-muntz) Final Four. Wade was named an All-American.

During the tournament, Wade led the Golden Eagles to an upset win over No. 1

Kentucky that ended the Wildcats' 26-game winning streak. He had a triple double, which means he got double digits in scoring (29 points), rebounds (11), and assists (11). It was only the ninth triple double in the 64-year history of the tournament.

Some experts said Wade should give up his final year of college and turn pro. After a lot of thought, Wade decided he was ready for the next level.

NBA **scouts** called Wade a top-10 pick. The No. 1 **prospect** (PRAH-spekt) was Cleveland high school senior LeBron James. The Cleveland Cavaliers chose him first. After Detroit chose Darko Milicic and Denver picked Carmelo Anthony, Toronto chose Georgia Tech's Chris Bosh. Next up was Miami, and the Heat chose Dwyane Wade. In his first four years he made $2.6 million, $2.8 million, $3.0 million, and $3.8 million. Since then he hasn't made less than $13 million a year.

By 2011, Wade was a seven-time **NBA All-Star** and had won an NBA scoring title (30.2 points in 2009). He was popular with fans. His

Wade chose number 3 for his jersey because it represents the Holy Trinity (the **Christian** Father, Son, and Holy Ghost).

jersey (No. 3) was sold the most in NBA stores from 2005 to 2007.

In 2002, while still at Marquette, Wade married his childhood sweetheart, Siohvaughn Funches. That year their first child, Zaire, was born. In 2007 another son, Zion, was born.

Germany couldn't stop Wade (#9) and the rest of Team USA, also called the Redeem Team, in the 2008 Olympics in China. Wade was the leading scorer, and after defeating Spain, the U.S. won the gold medal.

"Throughout my life I've never been at a loss for nicknames," Wade wrote on his official site. "There's D-Wade and Flash. I love them both, but no label sounds as good to me as Daddy."

During this time Wade's mother, Jolinda, who had gone to prison for selling drugs, got past her problems. She became a devout Christian like Wade. In 2007 she became a minister. She works with homeless and troubled people in Chicago. According to her web site, she says, "If God could take [me] from the gutter to the uttermost, then He can do it for anybody."

Wade also played on the U.S. 2004 Olympic team that won the bronze medal. When he and Team USA returned to the Olympics in 2008, they felt they had to **redeem** themselves. Wade led the Olympic team in scoring, averaging 16.0 points, 4.0 rebounds, and 2.3 steals. He had a game-high 27 points in the final game over Spain. After winning the gold medal, the U.S. was called the Redeem Team.

Miami fans were excited when superstars LeBron James (right) and Chris Bosh (center) joined Wade and the Heat. The players promised to bring the city an NBA championship, and they nearly did their first year.

# Sharing the Glory

During the 2008 Olympics, Wade became friends with fellow U.S. players LeBron James and Chris Bosh. They joked that they should play for the same NBA team so that they could win a bunch of championships. After a while, they stopped joking and started planning.

First, in the summer of 2010, Wade had to decide his future. He was a free agent, which meant he could sign with any team. The Heat wanted to keep him. They launched a We Want Wade **Campaign** (kam-PAYN) and made a web site for fans. It gave tips for how to show their support, like sending dessert to Wade's table at a restaurant or giving him a standing **ovation** (oh-VAY-shun) when they saw him. "We want to show Wade the love," the web site said. It worked. He stayed in Miami.

Then Bosh signed with the Heat. Finally, LeBron James left his hometown of Cleveland (making a lot of Cleveland fans very upset) to join Miami. The Heat talked about winning the NBA championship. Many people saw them as cocky and wanted them to lose.

Miami struggled early in the 2010–2011 season, then began to play well. Wade and James made the NBA All-Star team. Wade averaged 25.5 points during the season (his career average was 25.4), and 24.5 in the playoffs. James averaged 26.7 points during the season (career average of 27.8), and 23.7 in the playoffs.

Wade played well despite suffering from **migraine** (MY-grayn) headaches. They were so bad they made him sick and unable to see. Sometimes light could trigger one of these headaches, so he wore dark goggles during games.

The Heat reached the NBA finals, where they lost to Dallas in six games. Some people said they got what they deserved. Wade said they would do better next season.

During this time Wade and his wife divorced. For a while their sons lived with their mother in Chicago. In 2011, they came to live with their father. That made him very happy. "Since my sons came to live with me," he wrote in a Father's Day letter in *Newsweek*, "every day has been like Father's Day."

Dwyane has always been a good father to his sons, Zion (in his arms) and Zaire. He was named a 2007 *Men's Health* Father of the Year.

Jolinda Wade cut the ribbon to celebrate the opening of the building her son bought for her church in 2008. She overcame a drug addiction and jail time to become a Christian and then a minister. She started Temple of Praise Church in Chicago, and Dwyane pledges 10 percent of his salary to it.

**CHAPTER FIVE**

# Role Model

Wade has always cared about others. It was one of the first things Tom Crean noticed about him. "He can make you feel like you're the only one who is there, like you're the only one he is talking to," Crean said. "He's very **sincere** [sin-SEER] with that."

*Sports Illustrated* named Wade its Sportsman of the Year in 2006. He was just the sixth NBA player to win the honor, joining Bill Russell (1968), Kareem Abdul-Jabbar (1985), Michael Jordan (1991), and Tim Duncan and David Robinson (2003).

Wade says his dream is to "leave the world a better place than I found it." That's why

Wade is disguised as an employee to promote Gatorade in a sporting goods store. A lot of companies pay him to advertise their products. Besides Gatorade, he has deals with Lincoln, Staples, Sean John, T-Mobile, and Topps cards. He had his own line of shoes with Converse called The Wade, and T-Mobile made a D-Wade Edition of Sidekick phones.

he started the Wade's World Foundation to help education, health, and family service programs.

He joined former NBA player Alonzo Mourning to form the Athletes Relief Fund for Haiti to help the victims of that country's 2010 earthquake. He hosted A Week of Wade's World in South Florida for kids. It included a basketball camp, school supply shopping, and

Three years after Hurricane Katrina destroyed homes in New Orleans, Wade went door to door to hand out survival kits to local residents. His foundation planned to rebuild three homes there as well.

granting the wishes of Make-A-Wish children. He provides 10 tickets a year to every Heat home game for child-focused groups in Miami. In 2006, he hired two buses to take a hundred children from Miami to Disney World. They spent all day at the park, and he paid for everything. In 2008 he bought a new home for a South Florida family after a nephew accidentally burned down their home right

Wade enjoys teaching kids how to improve their basketball skills.

before Christmas. He presented it to them along with furniture, clothing, and gifts to make sure they had a special Christmas.

Wade has been successful in all of this because he wants to be the best. Tom Crean explained it this way: "He's got an uncommon drive. There are not a lot of us that have the drive he has to be successful the way he wants to be and along the way make everybody around him better."

That's what superstars do. Dwyane Wade is a superstar's superstar.

## CAREER STATISTICS

| Year | Team | G | Min | FGM | 3PM | FTM | REB | STL | BLK | TO | AST | PTS |
|------|------|-----|--------|-------|-----|-------|-------|-----|-----|-------|-------|--------|
| '03-'04 | MIA | 61 | 2,129 | 371 | 16 | 233 | 247 | 86 | 34 | 196 | 275 | 991 |
| '04-'05 | MIA | 77 | 2,974 | 630 | 13 | 581 | 397 | 121 | 82 | 321 | 520 | 1,854 |
| '05-'06 | MIA | 75 | 2,892 | 699 | 13 | 629 | 430 | 146 | 58 | 268 | 503 | 2,040 |
| '06-'07 | MIA | 51 | 1,933 | 472 | 21 | 432 | 239 | 107 | 62 | 216 | 384 | 1,397 |
| '07-'08 | MIA | 51 | 1,954 | 439 | 22 | 354 | 214 | 87 | 37 | 224 | 354 | 1,254 |
| '08-'09 | MIA | 79 | 3,048 | 854 | 88 | 590 | 398 | 173 | 106 | 272 | 589 | 2,386 |
| '09-'10 | MIA | 77 | 2,792 | 719 | 73 | 534 | 373 | 142 | 82 | 252 | 501 | 2,045 |
| '10-'11 | MIA | 76 | 2,823 | 692 | 63 | 494 | 485 | 111 | 87 | 237 | 346 | 1,941 |
| Career | | 547 | 20,548 | 4,876 | 309 | 3,847 | 2,783 | 973 | 548 | 1,986 | 3,472 | 13,908 |

(G = Games played, Min = Minutes played, FGM = Field goals made, 3PM = Three-pointers made, FTM = Free throws made, REB = Rebounds, STL = Steals, BLK = Blocks, TO = Turnovers, AST = Assists, PTS = Points)

# CHRONOLOGY

**1982** Dwyane Tyrone Wade Jr. is born on January 17 in Chicago. His parents divorce.

**1996** He enters Richards High School in Oak Lawn, Illinois, near Chicago.

**2000** As a high school senior, Dwyane sets school records for points (676) and steals (106) in a season. He accepts a scholarship to Marquette University in Milwaukee, Wisconsin.

**2002** He marries Siohvaughn Funches. Their son Zaire Blessing Dwyane is born in February.

**2003** In March, Wade leads Marquette to a 27-6 record and the NCAA basketball tournament's Final Four. He is named an All-America. He decides to skip his senior year of college and enter the NBA Draft. In June, he is the fifth pick in the draft by the Miami Heat. He later makes the NBA's all-rookie team.

**2004** Wade makes his first NBA All-Star team.

**2005** His Miami Heat jersey becomes the biggest seller in the NBA—ahead of such stars as Kobe Bryant and Shaquille O'Neal.

**2006** In his third NBA season, Wade leads Miami to the NBA championship. The Heat beats the Dallas Mavericks four games to two. Wade is named the championship series most valuable player (MVP) after averaging 34.7 points, 7.8 rebounds, and 3.8 assists.

**2007** Marquette retires Wade's jersey at halftime of their game on February 3. Marquette usually honors only student athletes who have graduated, but makes a special case for Wade because of his NBA accomplishments. His mother, Jolinda, becomes a preacher. His son, Zion Malachi Airamis, is born in May.

**2008** Wade leads Team USA in scoring (16.0 points per game) as the Americans win the Olympic gold medal in Beijing, China. He also leads the NBA in scoring for the 2008–2009 season (30.2 points a game).

**2010** Dwyane and Siohvaughn divorce. Wade agrees to stay with Miami and signs a contract that pays him $14 million for the season. NBA All-Stars LeBron James and Chris Bosh also sign with the Heat, making it one of the favorites to win the NBA championship.

**2011** Dwyane's sons move in with him. President Barack Obama asks Wade to help lead a group that encourages fathers to be more involved in their children's lives.

# FIND OUT MORE

## Books

Keith, Ted. *Dwyane Wade* (World's Greatest Athletes). North Mankato, MN: Child's World, 2008.

Savage, Jeff. *Dwyane Wade* (Amazing Athletes). Minneapolis: Lerner Publishing, 2007.

Smallwood, John. *Dwyane Wade* (NBA Reader). New York: Scholastic, 2007.

Smithwick, John. *Meet Dwyane Wade: Basketball's Rising Star.* New York: Scholastic, 2007.

Stewart, Mark. *The Miami Heat.* Chicago: Norwood House, 2007.

## Works Consulted

Author interview with Tom Crean, December 15, 2010.

"Bryant Passes Wade for Top-selling Jersey at NBA Stores." *ESPN.com,* January 10, 2007. http://sports.espn.go.com/nba/news/story?id=2727029

Dwyane Wade: Dwyane Wade News and Photos. *Sun-Sentinel*, n.d. http://www.sun-sentinel.com/topic/sports/basketball/dwyane-wade-PESPT008417.topic

"Heat Launch Site Aimed at Keeping Wade." Associated Press, May 13, 2010. http://m.espn.go.com/nba/story?storyId=5185939&top&wjb

Hollinger, John. "Greatest Finals Performances." *ESPN Insider*, June 16, 2011. http://proxy.espn.go.com/nba/playoffs2008/columns/story?columnist=hollinger_john&page=FinalsPerformances-1

Mourning, Alonzo, with Dan Wetzel. *Resilience: Faith, Focus, Triumph.* New York: Balantine Books, 2008.

NBA Player Profile: Dwyane Wade. http://www.nba.com/playerfile/dwyane_wade/

Price, S.L. "Sportsman of the Year: Dwyane Wade." *Sports Illustrated*, December 11, 2006. http://sportsillustrated.cnn.com/2006/magazine/12/05/sportsman1211/index.html

Reynolds, Tim. "Bosh, Wade Held Out of Heat Practice." Associated Press, January 20, 2011.

——. "Dwyane Wade Gives Mom a Church." Associated Press, May 20, 2008. http://www.chicagodefender.com/article-893-dwayne-wade-gives-mom-a-church.html

# FIND OUT MORE

Richardson, Shandel. "Injuries Providing Heat's Role Players an Opportunity." *Orlando Sun-Sentinel*, January 21, 2011. http://articles.sun-sentinel.com/2011-01-21/sports/fl-heat-injuries-backup-0122-20110121_1_james-and-bosh-joel-anthony-erik-spoelstra

Shoals, Bethlehem, et al. *FreeDarko Presents: The Undisputed Guide to Pro Basketball History.* New York: Bloomsbury, 2010.

Simmons, Bill. *The Book of Basketball: The NBA According to The Sports Guy.* New York: Ballantine Books/ESPN Books, 2009.

Wade, Dwyane. "My Life as an NBA Superstar Single Dad." *Newsweek*, June 5, 2011. http://www.newsweek.com/2011/06/05/my-life-as-an-nba-superstar-single.html

## On the Internet

Official Miami Heat We Want Wade Campaign Headquarters
http://www.wewantwade.com/

Official Site of Dwyane Wade
http://www.bballone.com/dwyanew/dwaynewade.html

The Official Site of the Miami Heat
http://www.nba.com/heat/

Pastor Jolinda Wade Ministries
http://www.jolindawadeministries.org/

Wade's World Foundation
http://www.wadesworldfoundation.org/fromthefounder.php

# GLOSSARY

**average** (AV-rij)—To score a certain number per game.

**campaign** (kam-PAYN)—A series of actions done for a single purpose (such as keeping Dwyane Wade in Miami).

**championship** (CHAM-pee-un-ship)—The final game that determines the top team in a league.

**Christian** (KRIS-chun)—A person who believes that Jesus is the son of God.

**conference** (KON-fruntz)—A group of teams that play against one another.

**eligible** (EL-ih-jih-bul)—To be allowed by the rules to do something.

**free throw**—A shot taken from the free throw line after a foul. Each shot made is worth one point.

**migraine** (MY-grayn)—A painful headache.

**NBA All-Star**—Any of the best players in the NBA, as voted by the fans. The All-Stars get together at midseason to play a game that is mostly for fun.

**NBA**—National Basketball Association, the major professional basketball league in North America. It consists of 30 teams divided into two conferences (Eastern and Western) and six five-team divisions.

**NCAA Tournament** (TUR-nuh-munt)—The college basketball tournament held each March that determines the major college national championship teams.

**ovation** (oh-VAY-shun)—A round of loud applause (clapping and cheering) from a crowd.

**playoffs**—Games played between the best teams of the regular season; the playoff winners in each conference meet for the overall championship.

**potential** (poh-TEN-shul)—Possible but not realized ability and achievement.

**prospect** (PRAH-spekt)—A high school player who might be good enough to play in college.

**rebound** (REE-bownd)—Grabbing the ball after a missed shot.

**recruit** (ree-KROOT)—To try to convince someone to join a team or group.

**redeem** (ree-DEEM)—To make up for a loss or mistake.

**resilience** (ree-ZIL-yuntz)—Ability to bounce back.

**scout** (SKOWT)—A person who watches players to see if they are good enough to play at the next level.

**sincere** (sin-SEER)—Acting in a way you can trust.

**steal**—In basketball, to take the ball away from a player on the other team.

# INDEX